OLD AMERICA

Battlefields

Lynn Stone

Rourke Publications, Inc.
Vero Beach, FL 32964

© 1993 Rourke Publications, Inc.

All rights reserved. No part of this book may be reproduced or utilized in any form or by any means, electronic or mechanical including photocopying, recording or by any information storage and retrieval system without permission in writing from the publisher.

Edited by Sandra A. Robinson

PHOTO CREDITS
© Gene Ahrens: cover, 6, 16, 18, 19; © James P. Rowan: title page, 4, 10, 11, 12, 13, 20, 25, 26; © Reinhard Brucker: 8, 17; © Jerry Hennen: 15; © Marianne Austin-McDermon: 28; © Lynn M. Stone: 22, 24.

Library of Congress Cataloging-in-Publication Data

Stone, Lynn M.
  Battlefields / by Lynn Stone.
  p. cm. — (Old America)
  Summary: Describes some of the key events in the military history of the United states and the sites where these events took place.
  ISBN 0-86625-444-7
  1. Battlefields – United States – Guidebooks – Juvenile literature. 2. United States – History, Military – Juvenile literature. 3. United States – Guidebooks – Juvenile literature. [l. United States – History, Military.] I. Title. II. Series: Stone, Lynn M. Old America.
E159.S79 1993
973—dc20   93-6781
                                                        CIP
                                                         AC

Printed in the USA

TABLE OF CONTENTS

I.	America's Battlefields	4
II.	Colonial Battlefields	8
III.	Wars with England and Mexico	13
IV.	The Civil War	16
V.	Wars with Native Americans	22
VI.	Battlefields: A Tour	26
	Glossary	30
	Index	31

I AMERICA'S BATTLEFIELDS

These "weekend soldiers," dressed in Confederate Army gray, are only re-enacting war, but for many years warfare on American soil was the real thing.

From sea to shining sea, America is a nation with a violent past. For nearly 400 years after the arrival of Europeans, American soil was bloodied by European nations and tribes of native peoples. Hundreds of battles were fought between competing nations, between nations and tribes, and between tribes. Soon after the first English **colonists** arrived in America, they battled French, Spanish and Native Americans. English colonists eventually fought against England itself for the right to establish a free nation, the United States. Over the years, the new states fought England again in the War of 1812. There were quarrels with Mexico over land. Finally, there was the horror of the Civil War.

During the centuries, battles erupted from disputes of ownership, greed, hate, vengeance, injustice and misunderstanding. Whatever their causes, the wars produced terror, death and tremendous suffering. They also produced major changes, for better or worse, in people's living conditions and in the borders of nations.

Battles reshaped the United States. Battlefields scattered throughout America are among the nation's most important **historic** sites. They are places where events occurred that changed the path of history — places with names like Saratoga, Yorktown, San Jacinto, Cold Harbor, Vicksburg, Gettysburg, Shiloh, Chickamauga, Antietam, the Little Bighorn and Fort Sumter. They are silent reminders of terrible events that happened long ago. There are open fields where soldiers stood fighting

This sunken road near Sharpsburg, Maryland, became known as Bloody Lane during the Battle of Antietam. A Union officer reported that the ground was so solidly covered with the dead that a person could walk across the lane on the bodies and never touch the ground.

shoulder-to-shoulder. There are rugged mountains, lakeshores, swamps, forts, villages, forests and moonlike landscapes of volcanic rock where battles were fought and men died.

Visitors to historic sites often find little to remind them of what really happened on the battlefields they can now safely walk. The shouts and screams of men, and the roar and smoke of guns and cannons are gone. The men themselves, their terror and their bravery, are left to our imaginations. Many battlefields, however, have monuments, exhibits, booklets and neat rows of white grave markers that give visitors some sense of what happened on those grounds.

II COLONIAL BATTLEFIELDS

Late in the French and Indian War, the British soldiers manning Fort Michilimackinac were all either captured or killed by Native Americans. Native Americans playing lacrosse outside the fort gates tricked the fort's guards.

The first waves of English colonists settled along the Atlantic coast of America in the 1600s. With England's help, the settlers established 13 colonies. To the west, French colonists settled along the St. Lawrence River and around the Great Lakes.

In Europe, Roman Catholic France and Protestant England were at war more often that not. Their bitter feelings carried into the New World. Both France and England wanted to expand their holdings and profits in North America. They fought an on-again-off-again war in North America between 1689 and 1763. When both France and England claimed a huge tract of land west of the Allegheny Mountains, fighting raged during what became known as the French and Indian War (1754-1763). Both sides had Native American **allies** who joined their cause.

The French and Indian War determined whether French or English culture would dominate North America. England won the war, and France surrendered Canada and nearly all of her lands east of the Mississippi River. Still, peace did not last.

By the 1760s, American colonists were finding increasing fault with England. The English government of King George III was far away, but it was still making laws and forcing the colonists to abide by them. Colonists disliked having British **troops**, the red-coated soldiers, stationed in their towns. They disliked paying

English taxes. They resented being told they could not settle west of the Appalachian Mountains. Finally, the arguments overheated. On April 19, 1775, American and British troops battled each other at Lexington and Concord, in the state of Massachusetts. Those battles began the Revolutionary War, which was fought largely in the American East. The colonists' goal was simple: independence.

The army of colonials never amounted to more than 20,000 men — far fewer than the British army in North America. Nevertheless, the Americans had more "stomach" for the war than the British, who had problems of

In a Revolutionary War re-enactment, men wear the uniforms of George Washington's Continental American Army.

At Lexington, Massachusetts, on April 19, 1775, Captain Parker told his American troops: "Stand your ground. Don't fire unless fired upon. But if they mean to have a war, let it begin here."

their own in Europe. Led by the brilliant George Washington and military leaders like Francis Marion and Casimir Pulaski, the colonists overcame disease, poor clothing and poor food. They also received help from France, always eager for battle with Great Britain.

The surrender of a British army unit at Saratoga, New York, in 1777 was a major stride toward victory for the colonists. When the Americans forced another British surrender at Yorktown, Virginia, in 1781, they brought the war to a finish — and gained independence.

Field guns of the American Revolution stand quietly in the woods of Yorktown, Virginia, where Washington's American and French troops forced a British surrender. Yorktown was the last major battle of the war.

No one knows how many American soldiers died in the Revolution. Estimates range from 5,000 to 25,000. Whatever the actual number, it was tiny in comparison to what lay ahead.

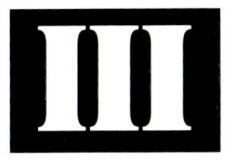

III WARS WITH ENGLAND AND MEXICO

Andrew Jackson's American troops fought from these defenses at the Chalmette Plantation and slaughtered attacking British soldiers in the Battle of New Orleans in January, 1815.

By 1812, American anger with England was again at a boil. England had interfered with American shipping and had been helping Native Americans resist American settlement west of the Appalachians. Great Britain agreed to stop interfering with American shipping. However, the agreement reached the United States two days *after* war had been declared. It was too late.

So began the strange War of 1812, a war in which neither side won anything. America's invasion of British-owned Canada failed badly. When the war ended, early in 1815, both sides declared victory and returned to their prewar borders. In another strange twist, the greatest American victory of the war occurred on January 8, 1815, in New Orleans, Louisiana — after the war had officially ended! England and the United States had agreed to peace, but no one on the battlefield knew it. In 1815 news seemed to travel on a tortoise's back.

While peace returned to the United States, American settlers in Mexico-owned Texas grew increasingly restless. In 1835, Texans of American and Mexican descent decided to form an independent state. Mexico sent a 5,000-man army to Texas to protect its rights. In February, 1836, Mexican General Santa Anna trapped 187 Texans in the Alamo, an old Spanish mission. After 11 days of fighting, the only survivors among the defenders were two women, a boy and a baby.

One of America's most famous battlegrounds, the Alamo was the scene of furious fighting between Texans and the Mexican army in 1836.

Mexico's victory was costly, for it stirred Texas into war. General Sam Houston's Texans defeated the Mexican army at San Jacinto, and Texas won its independence. The United States renewed warfare with Mexico in 1846. Seeking to expand its territory in the Southwest, the U.S. used a Mexican attack on an Army unit as an excuse for all-out war. Suffering repeated losses, Mexico surrendered after the fall of Mexico City in 1848. The United States took possession of a huge new territory, including present-day Arizona, New Mexico and California.

IV THE CIVIL WAR

Cast larger than life, soldierly statues rise over the battlefield at Antietam. One hundred thousand men clashed in 14 hours of bloody fighting on September 17, 1862. By the time it was over, 23,000 had been killed or wounded on the bloodiest day of the war.

As the "land of the free," America had a major flaw. In the South, there were more than 3 million black slaves. The Southern states' **prosperity**, or wealth, was tied to the farming of sugar, cotton, tobacco and rice. Much of the farm labor was provided by slaves.

By 1860, the Southern states felt their way of life — basically their right to hold slaves — was being threatened by the North. Eleven southern states **seceded**, declaring themselves independent of the United States. They formed a new nation, the Confederate States of America. President Abraham Lincoln urged the southern states to return to the Union. Secession was not legal, he said. When the breakaway states ignored the president, Lincoln, true to his word, used force to end the rebellion.

Like these re-enactment soldiers, Confederate and Union soldiers often stood in plain sight of each other's weapons.

Nearly 24,000 men were killed, wounded or missing after the great Civil War battle here at Shiloh in Tennessee.

    The American Civil War — also known as the War Between the States — erupted on April 12, 1861, and lasted four years. It was a war of incredible bloodshed, horror, misery and courage. Brothers, cousins and friends found themselves in opposing armies. The cost in lives was greater than any other war in which America has fought. More than 620,000 men died, about half of them from disease. One out of every three Confederate soldiers died. Nearly as many men died in the Civil War as in all of America's other wars combined.

    The battles were fought largely on Confederate territory, from Virginia and Maryland west to Tennessee, and south into the Carolinas, Mississippi and Georgia. The war's most important battle, however, was fought at Gettysburg, Pennsylvania in 1863. There Robert E. Lee's Confederate Army of 65,000 men tried once more to invade the North and threaten Washington, D.C. Eighty-five thousand Union soldiers resisted Lee. In three days of unbelievably brutal war, rifles, cannon fire, **bayonets** and **mortars** killed or wounded 40,000 men. Lee was forced to retreat, and the South's chances of winning independence were gone.

The Civil War was filled with the battles involving thousands of men fighting in open spaces. At Antietam, Maryland, nearly 25,000 were killed or wounded in a

Gettysburg National Military Park marks the site where Union forces stopped General Robert E. Lee's invasion of the North in three days of battlefield horror.

Soldiers at peace, many of them unknown, rest in this national military cemetery near Fort Donelson National Battlefield, scene of a Union victory in 1862.

single day of combat in 1862. Throughout the war, commanders spent their men like small coins. In 1864, at Cold Harbor, Virginia, Union General Ulysses Grant ordered a charge toward Confederates in trenches. Seven thousand Union soldiers were cut down in minutes. Grant should have known better. A year earlier at Gettysburg, Union troops had slaughtered many of the 13,000 Rebels who had charged their dug-in positions on Cemetery Ridge.

Lee's surrender at Appomattox Court House on April 9, 1865, brought this great national disaster to an end. The Civil War had established two guiding principles:

no state had the right to secede, and no person had the right to keep another as a slave.

The "house divided," as Lincoln called the nation, began its reunion.

V. WARS WITH NATIVE AMERICANS

Seminoles, hiding in these Florida pines, ambushed and massacred Major Francis Dade and nearly his entire force of about 100 men on December 28, 1835. The incident touched off the Second Seminole War in Florida.

Conflicts with Native Americans began almost immediately after the first European ships reached North America in 1492. Fighting lasted for nearly 400 years, as tribe after tribe refused to give up its land. Native Americans had been on North American soil for many thousands of years. When Native American groups did not willingly trade or sell their lands, settlers and armies took the land by force in battles such as Tippecanoe, Fort Recovery, Big Hole and the Washita.

Large-scale wars between whites and Native Americans were uncommon, and the battles were usually restricted to a small area. Native Americans rarely had the firepower of their white enemies. They fought hit-and-run battles and often attacked from ambush. **Massacres**, fights in which one force wiped out another, helped create hatred on both sides. Native American raiders sometimes surprised and killed mail riders, miners and helpless settlers in remote places. In turn, whites slaughtered Native Americans of all ages in their villages.

Native American warfare east of the Mississippi River ended by 1815. As settlements pushed westward — especially after the Civil War — the Native Americans of the plains fought desperately, but unsuccessfully. White men killed the buffalo that the Native Americans needed for food. Retreats and **reservations** (lands set aside for the tribes) became a way of life for

Prairie grasses sway over the Montana hills where General George A. Custer was defeated by Sioux and Cheyenne warriors at the Battle of the Little Bighorn in 1876.

Native Americans. In 1877, Chief Joseph of the Nez Perce tribe saw the situation clearly. "I see the whites all over the country gaining wealth," he said, "and see their desire to give us lands which are worthless."

One of the most famous battles in American history was won by Native Americans using superior numbers and firepower. It is popularly known as Custer's Last Stand, or the Battle of the Little Bighorn. The last great army of Native Americans, perhaps 2,000 of them, trapped General George A. Custer and his **cavalry** troops — some 225 horse-mounted soldiers — near the Little Bighorn River in Montana. Custer and all of his men died. Excavations are still going on at the site. History has still not come to the final decision as to what happened during the battle.

Custer's troopers of the Seventh Cavalry were outfitted like this actor.

After Custer's defeat, soldiers poured into Montana. The Sioux and Cheyenne who did not escape to Canada were herded onto reservations. The wars with Native Americans were nearly at an end. The final surrender of Geronimo's tiny Apache band in Arizona in 1886 ended fighting in the Southwest. The needless slaughter of Sioux by Army troops at Wounded Knee Creek in 1890 brought a sad history of frontier war to a close.

VI BATTLEFIELDS: A TOUR

Vicksburg National Military Park is the historic site of the six-week attack on Vicksburg, Mississippi, by Union troops in 1863.

America's National Park Service has established 15 national battlefields and nine national military parks. Several other battlegrounds are protected by states and other agencies. At some battlefields, the fights are re-enacted by hundreds of men. These "weekend soldiers" dress in old uniforms and carry old firearms. Their make-believe battles are called **re-enactments**. One of the best is in Selma, Alabama, where men in blue and gray re-enact the Civil War Battle of Selma.

Among the battlefields protected by the National Park Service are the following:

Colonial times and the French and Indian War are remembered at Fort Necessity, Pennsylvania. Several sites marking Revolutionary War battles include Minute Man Historic Park, Massachusetts; Cowpens Battlefield, South Carolina; Colonial Historic Park, Virginia; and Saratoga Historic Park, New York.

Palo Alto National Historic Site in Texas recalls the first major battle of the Mexican War. The Little Bighorn Battlefield is the site of Custer's defeat.

The National Park Service maintains Civil War battlefields in 10 states, preserving sites such as Chickamauga, Antietam, Vicksburg, Wilson's Creek, Gettysburg, Shiloh, Fredericksburg, Chancellorsville and Manassas (Bull Run).

The Robert Scruggs home still stands at Cowpens, South Carolina, where the American Army routed a 1,300-man British force during a Revolutionary War battle.

Part of the battlefield at Gettysburg, Pennsylvania was set aside as a national cemetery in November, 1863. Earlier that year, thousands of Americans from the North and South had been killed there in three furious days of fighting. At the cemetery, President Abraham Lincoln delivered the short speech that became known as the Gettysburg Address. In recalling the soldiers' brave stand, Mr. Lincoln said that the

28

nation "can never forget what they did here ..." The grounds of Gettysburg and dozens of other battle sites help us to remember.

GLOSSARY

allies (AL lies) - those who join others in a common cause

bayonet (bay un ET) - a steel blade attached to the muzzle of a rifle

cavalry (KAV ul ree) - a group of soldiers mounted on horses

colonist (KAHL un ihst) - a person who settles in a country that is different from the one in which he was born, such as a colonist from England settling in the colony of Virginia

historic (hiss TOR ihk) - something of importance in history

massacre (MASS uh ker) - an act of complete destruction, often involving helpless people

mortar (MOR ter) - a type of cannon with a short barrel

prosperity (prahs PAIR uh tee) - the condition of being successful, especially in gaining wealth

re-enactment (ree en AKT ment) - the re-creating of a historical event in order to educate or entertain

reservation (rez er VAY shun) - land set aside by government for use by a particular group, such as Native Americans

secede (seh SEED) - to withdraw from an organization

troops (TROOPS) - soldiers

INDEX

Alamo, the 14
Allegheny Mountains 9
Antietam 5, 19, 27
Apache 25
Appalachian Mountains 10, 14
Appomattox Court House 20
Arizona 15, 25
battlefields, national 27
bayonets 19
Big Hole, Battle of the 23
British army 10, 11
buffalo 23
Bull Run (see Manassas)
California 15
Canada 9, 14, 25
cavalry 24
Cemetery Ridge 20
Chancellorsville 27
Cheyenne 25
Chickamauga 5, 27
Civil War 5, 18, 19, 20, 23, 27
Cold Harbor, VA 5, 20
Colonial Historic Park 27
colonists 5, 9, 10, 11
Concord, MA 10
Confederate Army 19
Confederate soldiers 18
Confederate States of America 17
Cowpens Battlefield 27
Custer, General George A. 24, 25
Custer's Last Stand (see Little Big Horn, Battle of the)
England (see Great Britain)
English colonists 5, 9
Europe 9, 11
farming 17
Fort Necessity 27
Fort Recovery, Battle of 23
Fort Sumter 5
France 9, 11

Fredericksburg 27
French and Indian War 9, 27
French colonists 9
Georgia 19
Geronimo 25
Gettysburg Address 28
Gettysburg, PA 5, 19, 20, 27, 28, 29
Grant, General Ulysses 20
grave markers 7
Great Britain 5, 9, 11, 14
Great Lakes 9
Houston, General Sam 15
Joseph, Chief 24
King George III 9
Lee, General Robert E. 19, 20
Lexington, MA 10
Lincoln, Abraham 17, 21, 28
Little Bighorn, Battle of the 5, 24
Little Bighorn Battlefield 27
mail riders 23
Manassas 27
Marion, Francis 11
Maryland 18, 19
massacres 23
Mexican War 27
Mexico 5, 14, 15
Mexico City 15
military parks, national 27
miners 23
Minute Man Historic Park 27
Mississippi 19
Mississippi River 9, 23
Montana 24, 25
monuments 7
mortars 19
Native Americans 5, 14, 23, 24, 25
New Mexico 15
New Orleans, LA 14

31

New York 11
Nez Perce 24
North 17, 19, 28
Palo Alto National Historic Site 27
Pulaski, Casimir 11
re-enactments 27
reservations 23, 25
Revolution (see Revoluntionary War)
Revolutionary War 10, 12, 27
San Jacinto 5, 15
Santa Anna, General 14
Saratoga 5, 11
Saratoga Historic Park 27
Selma, AL 27
Selma, Battle of 27
settlers 9, 14, 23
Shiloh, TN 5, 27
Sioux 25
slaves 17
South 17, 19, 28
South Carolina 27
Southwest 15, 25
St. Lawrence River 9
Texas 14, 15
Tippecanoe, Battle of 23
U.S. National Park Service 27
Union soldiers 19, 20
Vicksburg 5, 27
Virginia 11, 18, 20
War Between the States (see Civil War)
War of 1812 5, 14
Washington, D.C. 19
Washington, George 11
Washita, Battle of the 23
Wilson's Creek 27
Wounded Knee Creek 25
Yorktown, VA 5, 11